THAI
COOKING

PARRAGON

THAI
COOKING

Photography by Peter Barry
Recipes by Jacqueline Bellefontaine
Designed by Claire Leighton and Helen Johnson
Edited by Jillian Stewart and Kate Cranshaw

4076
© 1994 Coombe Books
This edition published 1994 for Parragon Book Service Ltd.,
Unit 13-17, Avonbridge Trading Estate, Atlantic Road, Avonmouth,
Bristol BS11 9QD
All rights reserved.
Printed in Hong Kong
ISBN 1-85813-563-X

Contents

Introduction

Thailand is an amalgam of Indian and Chinese cultures and the cooking reflects these influences. The fiery spices of India are combined with the quick-cooking methods of Chinese cuisine, and added to these two elements are Thailand's own special ingredients such as coconut and lemon grass, fish sauce and curry paste – all of which result in the exciting flavours so typical of this country's distinctive cuisine.

A Thai meal is usually made up of at least five savoury dishes accompanied by rice. The various dishes may well include a soup, a sate, a curry, a vegetable dish with sauce and a noodle dish. The helpings of each dish are relatively small, in order that one may taste each one. The Thai people always pay great attention to the presentation of their food, serving each dish with a flourish of chopped coriander – an important and very common ingredient – or adorned with a beautifully fashioned spring onion in the shape of a delicate flower.

It is little wonder that Thai food is becoming more and more popular in Western countries. As well as guaranteeing delicious and stimulating flavours, it is quick to prepare and cook, with many dishes taking only minutes to produce from start to finish. It is also a healthy cuisine in which fresh vegetables, served raw or only lightly cooked, play a predominant part, and fish and chicken are more important components than red meats. The astounding growth in popularity of Thai cooking means that most Thai ingredients are now quite readily available at good supermarkets, as well as your nearest Oriental food store.

The most commonly used utensil in Thai cooking is a wok with a lid. Although you can use a large frying pan, as long as you cook on gas it is worthwhile investing in this inexpensive piece of equipment. If you cook on electricity a wide, flat-bottomed pan with a lid will be more effective than a wok. The secret of good stir-frying is to cook the foods quickly over a high heat, keeping the food constantly on the move to prevent it from burning. The high sides of a wok allow this to happen without the food being pushed out of the pan. The ingredients should be added in quick succession, so it is essential to prepare all the ingredients for the recipe before beginning to cook. For steaming, a bamboo steamer, which is placed directly in the wok, is needed.

Thai cooking's easy, relaxed style makes it a perfect cuisine for informal entertaining. So buy in the essential ingredients, arm yourself with a wok and steamer, and try some of these delicate and highly appetising recipes.

CHICKEN COCONUT SOUP

*This is a rich aromatic soup, and its mild flavour makes it particularly popular
with those new to Thai food.*

SERVES 4

1 chicken breast, skinned and boned
420ml/¾ pint thick coconut milk
280ml/½ pint chicken stock
6 slices galangal
2 red chillies, seeded and cut into strips
6 black peppercorns, crushed
4 kaffir lime leaves, torn in half
1 stem lemon grass, bruised
60ml/4 tbsps fish sauce
60ml/4 tbsps lime juice

1. Cut the chicken into thin strips across the grain.

2. Combine the coconut milk and chicken stock in a large saucepan and bring to the boil.

3. Reduce the heat to a simmer and add the sliced chicken, galangal, chillies, peppercorns, lime leaves and lemon grass.

4. Simmer gently for 15-20 minutes, or until the chicken is tender and cooked through.

5. Add the fish sauce and lime juice and serve.

TIME: Preparation takes 10-15 minutes and cooking takes about 20 minutes.

PREPARATION: To make the chicken easier to slice, partially freeze it so that it holds its shape to allow thin and even strips to be cut.

BUYING GUIDE: Galangal and either fresh or dried Kaffir lime leaves are available from Thai and Oriental food stores. If unavailable, substitute fresh root ginger and strips of lime zest.

COOK'S TIP: Canned coconut milk separates into two layers: a thick top 'cream' and a 'thin milk' underneath. If stirred together, these form 'thick milk'. Use whichever part the recipe requires, any excess can be frozen.

RICE SOUP WITH PORK

This dish often forms part of Thai breakfasts. Sometimes an egg is lightly poached in the soup just before serving.

SERVES 4

2 tbsps oil
2 cloves garlic, chopped
850ml/1½ pints pork or chicken stock
225g/8oz minced pork
340g/12oz cooked rice
2 sticks celery, sliced
2 spring onions, sliced
1 tbsp chopped fresh coriander leaves and
    stem
1 tbsp fish sauce
Pinch white pepper

1. Heat the oil in a small frying pan or wok and fry garlic until pale golden. Remove with a slotted spoon and drain on kitchen paper.

2. Put the stock in a large saucepan and bring to the boil, add the pork, rice, celery and spring onions and simmer gently for 15 minutes.

3. Stir in the coriander, fish sauce and pepper. Serve sprinkled with the fried garlic.

TIME: Preparation takes 10 minutes and cooking takes about 20 minutes.

VARIATION: Use chicken instead of pork and chop finely by hand or in a food processor.

COOK'S TIP: Cooked rice freezes very well, and can be quickly reheated in boiling water or by microwaving or steaming.

BEEF NOODLE SOUP

You can use any type of noodle in this recipe – substitute rice or cellophane noodles for a change.

SERVES 4

2 tbsps oil
225g/8oz sirloin steak, cut into thin strips
1 small onion, chopped
2 sticks celery, sliced diagonally
1.4 litres/2½ pints chicken or beef stock
1 tbsp chopped fresh coriander root and stem
2 Kaffir lime leaves
2.5cm/1-inch piece fresh root ginger, peeled and thinly sliced
1 tsp palm sugar
1 tbsp fish sauce
90g/3oz egg noodles
120g/4oz canned straw mushrooms (drained weight)

Garnish
Chilli 'flowers' (see Beef Sate recipe: PREPARATION)

1. Heat the oil in a wok or saucepan and fry the meat, onion and celery until the meat is cooked through and the vegetables are soft.

2. Add the stock, coriander, lime leaves, ginger, sugar and fish sauce. Bring to the boil.

3. Add the noodles and straw mushrooms and cook for 10 minutes. Serve piping hot, garnished with chilli 'flowers'.

TIME: Preparation takes 15 minutes and cooking takes 20 minutes.

COOK'S TIP: Partially freeze the steak to make slicing easier. Cut across the grain to keep the meat tender.

BUYING GUIDE: Kaffir lime leaves can be bought, fresh or dried from Oriental food stores. If unavailable, substitute strips of lime zest.

GLASS NOODLE SOUP

This attractive soup contains spicy meatballs and, of course, the cellophane noodles which give the dish its name.

SERVES 4

---

2 tbsps oil

2 cloves garlic, sliced

60g/2oz dried cellophane noodles

225g/8oz skinned and boned chicken breast

2 tbsps green curry paste (see separate recipe)

2 tbsps fish sauce

3 tbsps cornflour

1 tbsp chopped fresh coriander leaves

1 litre/1¾ pints chicken stock

225g/8oz bok choy, shredded

4 spring onions, cut into 5cm/1-inch pieces

---

1. Heat the oil in a small frying pan or wok and fry the garlic until pale golden. Remove with a slotted spoon and drain on kitchen paper.

2. Place the noodles in a large bowl and cover with hot water, allow to soak until softened, then drain.

3. Cut the chicken into chunks, then place in a food processor with the curry paste, fish sauce, cornflour and coriander, and process until very finely minced.

4. Remove the mixture from the processor and shape into small balls.

5. Heat the stock in a large saucepan until boiling and add the meatballs. Cook for 10-15 minutes or until they rise to the surface.

6. Add the softened noodles, bok choy and spring onions and continue to cook for 5 minutes. Serve sprinkled with the fried garlic slices.

TIME: Preparation takes 15 minutes and cooking takes 15-20 minutes.

PREPARATION: The curry paste can be made in advance or a commercially prepared paste can be bought from large supermarkets and Oriental specialist shops.

BUYING GUIDE: Bok choy is a type of chinese cabbage and is sometimes available in large supermarkets. If unavailable, substitute ordinary Chinese cabbage. Cellophane noodles are transparent when dried and are made from mung bean flour.

Spring Rolls

Spring rolls have become so popular that they are now available at supermarket delicatessens. However, they are simple to make at home and will taste much better than the supermarket version.

MAKES ABOUT 12

2 tbsps oil
1 clove garlic, crushed
120g/4oz chopped pork
2 carrots, peeled and cut into thin sticks
2 sticks celery, cut into thin sticks
1 red or green chilli, chopped
4 spring onions, sliced
1 tsp grated fresh root ginger
1 tbsp chopped fresh coriander leaves
1 tsp fish sauce
60g/2oz noodles, cooked
About 12 spring roll wrappers
Oil, for deep frying

Garnish
Fresh coriander leaves

1. Heat the oil in a wok or frying pan and fry the garlic, pork, carrots, celery and chilli for a few minutes until the pork is cooked through and the vegetables are beginning to soften.

2. Stir in the spring onions, ginger, coriander, fish sauce and noodles; cook gently to heat through.

3. Place a spring roll wrapper on a work surface and position a small amount of the filling across one corner. Roll up, folding in the corners to completely enclose the filling. Fill one spring roll at a time and keep the remaining wrappers covered with a damp tea-towel to prevent them from drying out.

4. Just before serving, deep-fry the spring rolls in batches, cooking them for 3-4 minutes or until crisp and golden. Drain on kitchen paper and keep warm while the rest are being cooked. Serve garnished with fresh coriander.

TIME: Preparation takes 20 minutes and cooking takes 15-20 minutes.

SERVING IDEAS: Serve with Sweet Chilli Sauce.

VARIATION: Add chopped prawns to the filling or bean sprouts.

BUYING GUIDE: Fresh or frozen spring roll wrappers can be bought from Oriental food stores.

BEEF SATE

A very popular Thai dish which can be served as a light snack or as party food.

SERVES 4

225g/8oz sirloin steak
Grated rind and juice of 1 lime
1 tsp chopped fresh chilli
1 tbsp chopped fresh coriander leaves and
    stems
½ tsp ground turmeric
½ tsp ground cumin
2 tsps fish sauce
Oil, for brushing

Sate Sauce
90g/3oz unsalted roasted peanuts
1 small red chilli
Juice of 1 lime
¼ tsp ground cumin
¼ tsp ground coriander
2 tbsps thick coconut milk
2 tbsps oil
1 small onion, chopped
Dash of fish sauce
30-60ml/2-4 tbsps water

Garnish
Chilli 'flowers' and spring onion 'brushes'

1. Cut the sirloin steak into thin slices, across the grain, and thread onto bamboo skewers. Place in a shallow dish.

2. Mix together the lime rind and juice, chilli, coriander, turmeric, cumin and fish sauce and pour over the beef. Turn to coat in the marinade and leave for at least 1 hour.

3. To prepare the sauce, place the peanuts, chilli, lime juice, spices and coconut milk in a pestle and mortar or food processor and grind to a paste.

4. Heat the oil in a pan and fry the onion until soft. Stir in the peanut mixture and add some fish sauce to taste. Add any remaining marinade and a little water to form a thick sauce. Cook for 5 minutes, stirring constantly.

5. Remove skewers from the marinade, brush with oil and cook under a preheated grill for 3-5 minutes or until the beef is cooked through. Serve with sate sauce. Garnish with chillies and spring onions, see PREPARATION below.

TIME: Preparation takes 15 minutes plus 1 hour marinating and cooking takes 10 minutes.

PREPARATION: To make the garnish, slit the chillies open, lengthwise, at close intervals all the way round, keeping the stem end intact, stand in iced water until curled. To prepare the spring onions, slash the ends into fine strips and stand in iced water until curled.

VARIATION: Crunchy peanut butter can be used instead of ground peanuts.

SON-IN-LAW EGGS

This popular and well known Thai dish is traditionally made with duck eggs but hen eggs can be used.

SERVES 4

Sauce
140ml/¼ pint tamarind juice
75g/2½oz dark muscovado sugar
90ml/6 tbsps fish sauce

Oil, for deep frying
4 shallots, thinly sliced
4 cloves garlic, sliced
4 hard-boiled eggs, shelled

Garnish
Spring onion 'brushes' and chilli 'flowers',
    (see Beef Sate recipe: PREPARATION)

1. To make the sauce, combine the tamarind juice, sugar and fish sauce in a small saucepan and heat gently, stirring until sugar dissolves. Bring to the boil, then reduce the heat and simmer gently for 5-10 minutes.

2. Heat the oil in a wok to 180°C/350°F. Add the shallots and fry for 1-2 minutes, until golden brown and crisp. Remove with a slotted spoon and drain on kitchen paper.

3. Add the garlic and fry for 1 minute, or until golden, taking care not to allow it to burn. Drain on kitchen paper.

4. Add the eggs to the wok and deep-fry for 5-10 minutes, until golden and bubbly on all sides. Keep turning the eggs so that they do not burn on the bottom. When golden, remove from the oil and drain the eggs on kitchen paper.

5. Cut the eggs in half, lengthways and arrange on a serving dish. Sprinkle the fried shallots and garlic over the egg.

6. Serve the sauce in a separate bowl, or poured over the eggs. Garnish with spring onion brushes and chilli flowers.

TIME: Preparation takes 20 minutes and cooking takes 15-20 minutes.

WATCHPOINT: Allow the oil to cool in the wok before removing it.

PREPARATION: See recipe for Fried Fish with Tamarind for method of preparing tamarind juice. If unavailable, substitute lemon juice.

SPICY PRAWN WRAPS

Use large, uncooked deep-water prawns for this dish, look out for them in the freezer cabinet in Oriental shops.

SERVES 4

12 uncooked king prawns
1 clove garlic, crushed
1 stem lemon grass, soft core finely sliced
1 red chilli, seeded and chopped
1 tsp grated fresh root ginger
Juice of 1 lime
12 small spring roll wrappers
Oil, for deep-frying

1. Peel the prawns, removing their heads and body shells, but leaving the tail fins attached.

2. Remove the dark vein and 'butterfly' the prawns by cutting through the back of the prawns without cutting right through the bodies. Carefully open the prawns out.

3. Combine the garlic, lemon grass, chilli, ginger and lime juice in a shallow dish, and add the prawns.

4. Turn the prawns so that they are coated in the marinade, then allow to marinate in the refrigerator for 2 hours, turning occasionally.

5. Just before serving, remove the prawns from the marinade and wrap each prawn in a spring roll wrapper, leaving the tail end sticking out.

6. Heat the oil to 180°C/350°F in a wok and fry the prawn wraps in batches for 3-4 minutes or until golden. Drain on absorbent paper.

TIME: Preparation takes 20 minutes, plus 2 hours marinating. Cooking takes about 12 minutes.

COOK'S TIP: Keeping the tail fins on the prawns gives you something to hold on to when eating them.

SERVING IDEA: Serve with a hot dipping sauce such as Nuoc Cham, see separate recipe.

BUYING GUIDE: Fresh or frozen spring roll wrappers can be bought in Oriental food stores.

THAI OMELETTE

Serve this omelette for a fast luncheon dish or as a starter. In Thailand, it is always presented with a hot dipping sauce.

SERVES 2-4

6 eggs
2 tbsps fish sauce
1 tsp water
1 small red chilli, sliced
3 spring onions, sliced
2 tbsps oil

Garnish
Banana leaves
Chilli curls

1. Place the eggs in a mixing bowl with the fish sauce and water and whisk until well combined and slightly frothy.

2. Stir in the chilli and spring onions.

3. Heat the oil in a heavy-based frying pan and when a haze rises from the pan, pour in the egg mixture.

4. Reduce the heat and cook the egg mixture, pulling the egg from the side of the pan as it sets, and letting the uncooked mixture run to the edges of the pan.

5. When the egg mixture is almost set, place under a preheated grill to brown the top.

6. Slide onto a serving plate and cut into wedges. Garnish with shapes cut from a banana leaf and chilli curls. Serve with a dipping sauce.

TIME: Preparation takes 10 minutes and cooking takes about 10 minutes.

COOK'S TIP: The small chillies that are used in Thai cookery are called 'birds eye' chillies and are very hot.

THAI PORK STUFFED OMELETTES

A plain omelette is filled with a spicy pork mixture.

SERVES 2

Filling

2 tbsps oil

1 small green chilli, sliced

1 clove garlic, crushed

2 shallots, chopped

120g/4oz minced pork

30g/1oz peeled prawns, chopped

2 tbsps fish sauce

1 large plum tomato, chopped

2 tsps sugar

Pinch white pepper

2 tbsps chopped fresh coriander leaves, stem and root

Omelettes

4 eggs

1 tbsp fish sauce

1 tsp water

2 tbsps oil

Garnish

Chilli 'flowers' (see Beef Sate: PREPARATION)

1. To make the filling, heat the oil and fry the chilli, garlic and shallots for 3 minutes or until softened.

2. Add the minced pork and cook until it has changed colour, breaking it up as it cooks.

3. Add the remaining filling ingredients and stir-fry for 3-4 minutes, then remove from the wok and keep warm whilst cooking the omelette.

4. To make the omelettes, place the eggs in a mixing bowl with the fish sauce and water and whisk until well combined and slightly frothy.

5. Heat half the oil in a small heavy-based frying pan and when just hazing, pour in half the egg mixture.

6. Reduce the heat and cook the egg mixture, pulling the egg from the side of the pan as it sets, and letting the uncooked mixture run to the edges of the pan.

7. When the egg mixture is almost set, gently flip over to cook the top or place under a preheated grill to lightly brown.

8. Spoon half the pork mixture into the centre of the omelette then fold it up to completely enclose the filling. Transfer to a serving dish and repeat with the remaining egg and pork mixture. Serve with a dipping sauce and garnish with chilli 'flowers'.

TIME: Preparation takes 15 minutes and cooking takes 20-25 minutes.

COOK'S TIP: If you have two small frying pans cook both omelettes at once, or if wished, use one large frying pan and make one large omelette.

Sweet Prawn and Coconut Curry

A milder curry which is best served with plain Thai steamed rice.

SERVES 4

460g/1lb raw prawns, peeled
140ml/¼ pint thick coconut milk
2 tsps lime juice
2 tbsps oil
1 clove garlic, crushed
4 shallots, sliced
1 tbsp grated fresh root ginger
1 tbsp yellow curry paste, see separate
    recipe
5 tsps palm sugar

Garnish
Lemon and lime wedges
1 tbsp desiccated coconut, toasted

1. Combine the prawns, coconut milk and lime juice together in a shallow dish. Leave to marinate for at least 30 minutes, stirring occasionally.

2. Heat the oil in a wok and fry the garlic and shallots until softened.

3. Stir in the ginger and curry paste and stir-fry for 1-2 minutes. Stir in the sugar.

4. Add the prawns and their marinade to the wok and cook over a reduced heat for 5 minutes or until the prawns turn pink and are just cooked through.

5. Transfer to a serving dish and garnish with lemon and lime wedges. Sprinkle with coconut and serve immediately.

TIME: Preparation takes 10 minutes, plus at least 30 minutes marinating. Cooking takes about 10 minutes.

COOK'S TIP: The curry paste can be made in advance. If palm sugar is unavailable, use muscovado sugar.

BUYING GUIDE: Coconut milk can be bought canned from large supermarkets and Asian food stores. It is also available in a powdered, instant form.

SEAFOOD WITH EGG NOODLES

Use any mixture of seafood in this spicy dish, which can be served as a main meal.

SERVES 4

460g/1lb mixed seafood, such as prawns, chunks of fish, squid, clams and mussels
3 large green chillies, seeded and chopped
1 tbsp chopped fresh coriander leaves
2 cloves garlic, crushed
175g/6oz egg noodles
2 tbsps oil
120g/4oz mange tout peas
120g/4oz baby corn cobs
½ red pepper, sliced
1 tbsp fish sauce
140ml/¼ pint fish stock
1 tbsp lime juice
2 tsps cornflour

1. Cook the seafood separately in boiling water until cooked through, then drain and set aside.

2. Pound together the chillies, coriander and garlic in a pestle and mortar.

3. Cook the noodles as directed on the packet.

4. Heat the oil in a wok, fry the mange tout, baby corn and pepper for 4 minutes, add the chilli mixture and fish sauce and cook for 2 minutes.

5. Stir in the fish stock, add the cooked seafood and noodles to the pan. Mix the lime juice and cornflour together. Stir into the wok and cook until thickened.

TIME: Preparation takes 15 minutes and cooking takes about 15 minutes.

COOK'S TIP: If using squid, score the heads in a diamond pattern before cutting into pieces, to help keep it tender.

STEAMED FISH

Steaming is a particulary well suited method of cooking for fish as it does not destroy the flavour. The accompanying ingredients added immediately after cooking give this dish a distinct Thai flavour.

SERVES 4

460g/1lb white fish fillets, skinned
2 shallots, sliced
1 stem lemon grass, sliced
3 tbsps lime juice
2 tbsps fish sauce
1 tsp palm sugar
2 cloves garlic, chopped
1 red chilli, chopped
1 green chilli, chopped

1. Cut the fish into thick strips and place in a serving dish that will fit into the top of a steamer.

2. Scatter the sliced shallots and lemon grass over the fish and steam for 10 minutes or until fish is cooked through.

3. Meanwhile, combine the lime juice, fish sauce and sugar together in a small bowl, stir until the sugar dissolves.

4. Combine the garlic and chillies together in another small bowl.

5. As soon as the fish is cooked, remove from the steamer and pour the fish sauce mixture over it. Scatter the chilli and garlic mixture over the top and serve immediately.

TIME: Preparation takes 15 minutes, and cooking takes about 10 minutes.

COOK'S TIP: If wished, the seeds of the chillies can be removed for a milder flavour.

PREPARATION: When using lemon grass the tough outer leaves should be removed and only the central soft core should be chopped.

FRIED FISH WITH TAMARIND

In this dish the fish is served with a delicious sweet and sour sauce.

SERVES 2-4

2 × 460g/1lb whole fish, eg red snapper,
    pomfret or bream, cleaned

3 tbsps cornflour

Oil, for frying

2 cloves garlic, crushed

1 tbsp grated fresh root ginger

1 small red chilli, sliced

1 small green chilli, sliced

6 spring onions, sliced

1 tbsp soy sauce

2 tbsps palm sugar

2 tbsps fish sauce

140ml/¼ pint tamarind juice, see
    PREPARATION below

Garnish

Lemon twists

Coriander leaves

Sliced spring onion tops

1. Cut 2-3 slashes on each side of the fish and dredge with the cornflour.

2. Heat about 5cm/2-inches of oil in a wok and fry the fish one at a time for about 5 minutes on each side. When cooked, transfer to a serving dish and keep warm.

3. Pour off most of the oil from the wok and add the garlic, ginger, chillies and spring onions and stir-fry for 2-3 minutes.

4. Stir in the soy sauce, palm sugar and fish sauce and stir until the sugar dissolves.

5. Add the tamarind juice and heat through. Pour some of the sauce over the fish and serve the remainder separately. Garnish with lemon twists, coriander leaves and a pile of spring onion slices.

TIME: Preparation takes 15 minutes and cooking takes about 20 minutes.

PREPARATION: To prepare the tamarind juice, use 2½ tsps of instant or concentrated tamarind with 140ml/¼ pint warm water or soak 3½ tbsps of tamarind pulp in the warm water for 5 minutes. Squeeze and knead the pulp to extract all the juice and flavour, then strain the liquid and use as required.

BUYING GUIDE: Tamarind can be bought from Asian food stores. If unavailable, substitute lemon juice.

FISH CAKES

Fish cakes are just one of the delicious savouries that you can buy from street vendors in Bangkok, where they make and cook them while you wait.

MAKES 8

275g/10oz white fish fillets, skinned
3 tbsps red curry paste (see separate recipe)
2 tbsps fish sauce
3 tbsps cornflour
1 tbsp chopped fresh coriander leaves
2 spring onions, finely sliced
1 egg, beaten
Oil, for frying

Garnish
Carrot and spring onion strips

1. Place the fish, curry paste, fish sauce, cornflour and coriander in a food processor and process until very finely minced.

2. Remove the mixture from the processor and beat in the spring onions, adding enough egg to bind the mixture together.

3. Using dampened hands, shape the mixture into eight small rounds, then chill until required.

4. Shallow- or deep-fry for a few minutes until golden. Serve with a dipping sauce or chutney of your choice and garnish with strips of carrot and spring onion.

TIME: Preparation takes 10 minutes and cooking takes 5 minutes.

PREPARATION: Make the curry paste in advance.

STEAMED FISH IN BANANA LEAVES

Lining the steamer with banana leaves, as in Thailand, imparts extra flavour to this dish, but you can use foil or greaseproof paper instead.

SERVES 4

460g/1lb white fish fillets, skinned
Banana leaves
2 carrots, peeled and cut into thin sticks
1 red pepper, cut into strips
120g/4oz long beans or French beans, cut into 7.5cm/3-inch lengths
2 courgettes, cut into thin sticks
140ml/¼ pint thick coconut milk
1-2 tbsps red curry paste (see separate recipe)
2 Kaffir lime leaves
1 tbsp fish sauce

1. Cut the fish into bite-size pieces or strips about 1cm/½-inch wide.

2. Line a heat-proof dish, which will fit into your steamer, with banana leaves.

3. Blanch the carrots, pepper and beans for 2 minutes in boiling water, add the courgettes for 30 seconds then drain and scatter over the banana leaf.

4. Pile the fish on top of the vegetables.

5. Combine the remaining ingredients and pour over the fish. Cover the steamer and steam for 15-20 minutes or until the fish is cooked through and flakes easily.

TIME: Preparation takes 15 minutes and cooking takes 15 minutes.

BUYING GUIDE: Fresh Banana leaves are available from Thai and Oriental food stores. They are stored refrigerated and should be washed well before using. Kaffir lime leaves are also available fresh or dried, but if unobtainable substitute strips of lime zest.

STEAMED PRAWNS

Serve these simply prepared prawns with a rice dish such as Shrimp Paste Fried Rice and a hot dipping sauce.

SERVES 4

460g/1lb raw prawns
2 tbsps sesame oil
2 cloves garlic, chopped
2 tbsps chopped fresh coriander root, stem
    and leaves
2 tsps grated fresh root ginger
1 red chilli, sliced
1 green chilli, sliced
2 tbsps soy sauce

Garnish
Lemon and lime twists

1. Wash and peel the prawns.

2. Combine the remaining ingredients in a small jug.

3. Place the prawns in a bowl or plate that will fit into a steamer basket. Pour the sauce over and toss well.

4. Place the plate in the steamer, cover and steam for 15 minutes or until the prawns have turned pink and are cooked through.

5. Serve immediately, garnished with lemon and lime twists.

TIME: Preparation takes 15 minutes, and cooking takes about 15 minutes.

COOK'S TIP: If you can't buy fresh coriander with roots, just use the stems and leaves.

PREPARATION: Do not overcook the prawns as they will become tough.

STIR-FRIED SEAFOOD

Seafood plays a prominent part in Thai cooking especially in the south.

SERVES 4

---

1 tsp black peppercorns
1 shallot, chopped
2 small red chillies, sliced
3 cloves garlic, crushed
2 tbsps oil
225g/8oz peeled raw prawns
340g/12oz prepared mixed seafood eg.
    clams, squid, scallops etc
1 tbsp fish sauce
1 tbsp lime juice
4 spring onions, sliced

1. Place the black peppercorns in a pestle and mortar and crush well. Add the shallot, chillies and garlic and continue to pound until well combined.

2. Heat the oil in a wok, add the chilli mixture and fry for 1 minute.

3. Add the prawns and the other prepared seafood and stir-fry for 3-4 minutes or until cooked through.

4. Sprinkle with the fish sauce and lime juice. Serve scattered with spring onion slices.

TIME: Preparation takes 10 minutes, cooking takes 5-6 minutes.

COOK'S TIP: Prepared mixed seafood can be bought in some large supermarkets.

THAI SWEET SOUR FISH

Fish plays a very important part in Thai cuisine especially in the south. It is often fried in a wok and served with a hot sauce, as with this recipe.

SERVES 2

2 × 460g/1lb whole fish such as pomfret, snapper or bream, cleaned
Oil, for shallow frying
4 green chillies, seeded and sliced
2.5cm/1-inch piece fresh root ginger, peeled and cut into thin sticks
2 cloves garlic, crushed
1 carrot, peeled and cut into thin sticks
3 tbsps white wine vinegar
1 tbsp fish sauce
60g/4 tbsps dark muscovado sugar
60ml/4 tbsps fish stock
6 spring onions, shredded
1 tsp cornflour mixed with a little water

1. Cut several slashes in each side of the fish. Heat some oil in a wok or frying pan and fry the fish for about 5-10 minutes each side. Remove from the pan and keep warm while preparing the sauce.

2. Wipe out the pan and heat a little more oil in it. Fry the chillies, ginger, garlic and carrot for 3-4 minutes.

3. Stir in the vinegar, fish sauce, sugar and stock and bring to the boil. Add the spring onions.

4. Stir the cornflour and water into the wok and cook until sauce thickens. Pour over the fish to serve.

TIME: Preparation takes 15 minutes and cooking takes 20-25 minutes.

COOK'S TIP: The fish can also be grilled or barbecued over charcoal.

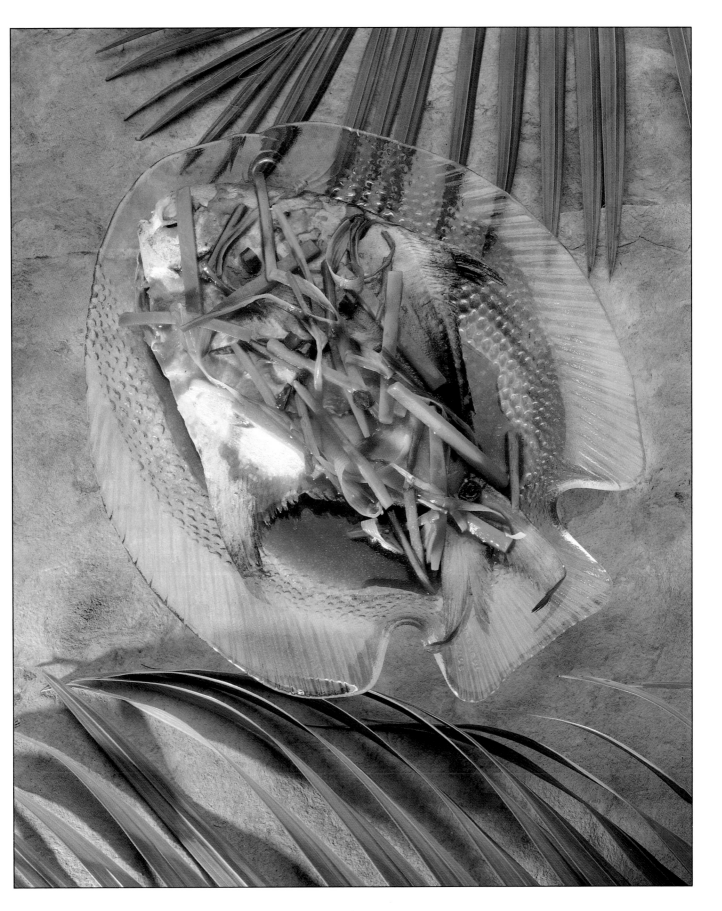

GREEN CURRY WITH BEEF

If you can not find small white aubergines (they are available in Asian food stores) substitute chunks of purple aubergine instead.

SERVES 4

2 tbsps oil

3 tbsps green curry paste (see separate recipe)

340g/12oz sirloin or rump steak, thinly sliced

420ml/¾ pint thick coconut milk

2 tbsps fish sauce

4 kaffir lime leaves, torn in half

8 small white aubergines, quartered

2 large red chillies, quartered lengthways

2.5cm/1-inch piece galangal, sliced

1 tsp palm sugar

1. Heat the oil in a wok and fry the green curry paste for 2 minutes, stirring frequently.

2. Add the beef and stir-fry for 2 minutes or until the meat changes colour.

3. Stir in the coconut milk and fish sauce and bring to the boil. Boil rapidly for 5 minutes, stirring occasionally.

4. Reduce the heat and stir in the lime leaves, aubergines, chillies, galangal, and sugar. Simmer for 5-10 minutes or until the aubergines are tender and serve with rice.

TIME: Preparation takes 15 minutes, and cooking takes 15-20 minutes.

COOK'S TIP: Partially freeze the beef to make cutting easier, and slice the meat across the grain. If palm sugar is unavailable, use muscovado sugar.

BUYING GUIDE: Galangal and Kaffir lime leaves (fresh and dried) can be bought in Asian food stores. If unavailable substitute fresh root ginger and strips of lime zest.

BEEF IN OYSTER SAUCE

You can make this spicy dish very quickly.

SERVES 4

460g/1lb sirloin steak
2 tbsps oil
¼ tsp ground cumin
¼ tsp ground coriander
175g/6oz baby corn cobs
120g/4oz can bamboo shoots, drained
175g/6oz mange tout peas
2 tbsps oyster sauce
2 tsps muscovado sugar
140ml/¼ pint beef stock
1 tsp cornflour
1 tbsp fish sauce

Garnish
Spring onion slices

1. Cut the beef into thin slices and then into strips.

2. Heat the oil in a wok and fry the beef over a high heat for 5 minutes or until cooked. Stir in the spices and cook for 1 minute.

3. Add the vegetables, then stir in the oyster sauce, sugar and stock, and bring to the boil.

4. Mix the cornflour with the fish sauce and stir into the pan, cooking until sauce thickens. Sprinkle with slices of spring onion to garnish.

TIME: Preparation takes 10 minutes and cooking takes 10 minutes.

COOK'S TIP: Partially freezing the beef will make it easier to cut. Slice into strips across the grain to keep the meat tender.

SPICY MINCED BEEF

A favourite dish in northern Thailand.

SERVES 4

1 tbsp glutinous rice
1 tbsp oil
1 stem lemon grass, sliced
4 small red chillies, sliced
2 cloves garlic, chopped
1 tbsp grated fresh root ginger
460g/1lb lean minced beef
Juice of 1 lemon
2 tbsps fish sauce
1 tbsp chopped fresh coriander leaves

Garnish
Lime wedges

1. Place the rice in a wok and dry-fry for 5-10 minutes until all the grains are golden on all sides, shaking the wok as it cooks.

2. Pour the toasted rice into a pestle and mortar and pound until ground almost to a powder.

3. Heat the oil in the wok, add the lemon grass, chillies, garlic and ginger, and stir-fry for 3 minutes.

4. Add the beef and cook until the meat changes colour, breaking it up as it cooks.

5. When the meat is cooked, sprinkle with the lemon juice and fish sauce. Stir in the ground up rice and cook for 1 minute.

6. Transfer to a serving dish and scatter with the coriander leaves. Garnish with lime wedges.

TIME: Preparation takes 15 minutes, and cooking takes 15-20 minutes.

BUYING GUIDE: Glutinous rice is available from Asian food stores.

PREPARATION: When using lemon grass, remove the tough outside leaves and only chop the soft inner core.

STEAMED PORK CUPS

This spicy pork mixture is served with a light salad and a hot dipping sauce.

SERVES 4-6

460g/1lb lean pork
5 cloves garlic, crushed
6 spring onions, sliced
2 green chillies, sliced
1 tbsp roasted cashew nuts
1 tsp shrimp paste
2 tbsps soy sauce
1 tbsp fresh coriander leaves and stem
Pinch white pepper
1 tsp palm sugar
120ml/4 fl oz thick coconut milk
2 egg whites

Salad

1 red pepper, sliced
1 green pepper, sliced
120g/4oz bean sprouts
2 tbsps lime juice
1 tbsp fish sauce

1. Cut away any fat from the pork and cut the meat into chunks. Place in a food processor and process briefly.

2. Add the garlic, spring onions, chillies, cashew nuts, shrimp paste, soy, coriander, pepper and sugar to the processor and process until all the ingredients are chopped and well combined.

3. Transfer the pork mixture to a bowl and beat in the coconut milk. Whisk the egg whites until standing in soft peaks, then fold into the mixture. Pile the pork mixture into small dishes. Place in a steamer and steam for 20 minutes, then remove from the steamer and allow to cool.

4. To make the salad, combine the peppers and bean sprouts and sprinkle with the lime juice and fish sauce.

5. Turn the pork out of the dishes and cut into wedges, serve with the pepper and bean sprout salad and a hot dipping sauce of your choice.

TIME: Preparation takes 20 minutes, and cooking takes about 20 minutes.

COOK'S TIP: Place a sheet of greaseproof paper or foil over the pork as it cooks, to prevent any condensation dripping into the dishes.

BUYING GUIDE: Shrimp paste, often known as blanchan, is available in blocks from Asian food stores. The colour varies from brown to pink, and it has a very pungent smell so must be stored in an airtight container.

PORK CURRY WITH AUBERGINE

This hot and spicy pork curry can be serve accompanied with rice for a delicious meal in itself.

SERVES 6

900g/2lbs belly pork strips

2 tbsps oil

3 tbsps red curry paste (see separate recipe)

570ml/1 pint water

120g/4oz sliced bamboo shoots

6 small white aubergines, quartered

90g/3oz long beans, cut into 2.5cm/1-inch pieces

3 large green chillies, seeded and quartered lengthways

2 tbsps fish sauce

1 tbsp lime juice

1 tsp palm sugar

Small bunch basil, torn into pieces

1. Remove the rind from the pork if wished and cut the meat into 2.5cm/1-inch slices.

2. Heat the oil in the wok and fry the curry paste for 2-3 minutes, add the meat and fry for 5 minutes.

3. Pour in the water and bring to the boil.

4. Reduce the heat and add the bamboo shoots, aubergines, long beans and chillies Simmer gently for 10 minutes.

5. Stir in the fish sauce, lime juice, sugar and basil and serve immediately.

TIME: Preparation takes 20 minutes, and cooking takes 25-30 minutes.

COOK'S TIP: Prepare the red curry paste in advance.

BUYING GUIDE: Small white aubergines and long beans can be found in Asian food stores. If unavailable substitute chunks of ordinary purple aubergine and French beans.

BARBECUED PORK

Traditionally this dish would be cooked on charcoal burners by the roadside, but it works just as well in the oven.

SERVES 4

4 cloves garlic, crushed
140ml/¼ pint light soy sauce
60g/2oz muscovado sugar
1 tbsp grated fresh root ginger
1 tbsp chopped fresh coriander stems and
   root
4 star anise or 1 tsp ground anise
Red food colouring (optional)
2 pork fillets
2 tbsps oil
2 shallots, chopped
120g/4oz roasted peanuts, ground
140ml/¼ pint pork or chicken stock
1 tsp cornflour mixed with a little water

Garnish
Kafffir lime leaves and star anise

1. Mix together the garlic, soy, sugar, ginger, coriander, anise and a few drops of food colouring to make a marinade.

2. Place the fillets in a shallow dish and add the marinade. Turn the pork over so that it is fully coated in the marinade. Leave to marinate for at least 1 hour, turning once.

3. Remove the meat from the marinade and place on a trivet in a roasting dish. Roast in a preheated oven, 375°F/190°C/Gas Mark 5, for 20 minutes or until pork is cooked. Baste once or twice with the marinade. Test the pork with a skewer – the juices should run clear.

4. Just before the end of the roasting time, heat the oil in a wok and fry the shallots until tender and beginning to brown. Stir in the ground peanuts, the marinade and stock. Cook until simmering, then add the cornflour mixture and cook a little longer until thickened.

5. To serve, slice the pork and pour the sauce over. Garnish with lime leaves and star anise.

TIME: Preparation takes 15 minutes, plus 1 hour marinating and cooking takes 20 minutes.

SERVING IDEAS: Serve with Thai Steamed Rice.

CHICKEN WITH CHILLI AND BASIL

Three kinds of basil are used in Thailand. Bai Horapa is the nearest to European basil. Look out for the other Thai varieties in Asian shops.

SERVES 4

4 chicken quarters
3 large red chillies, seeded and chopped
1 tbsp chopped fresh coriander root and stem
2 cloves garlic, crushed
3 tbsps oil
2 green chillies, sliced
2 tbsps fish sauce
1 tbsp oyster sauce (optional)
Small bunch basil, torn into small pieces

Garnish
Chilli 'flowers' (see Beef Sate recipe:
    PREPARATION)

1. Cut the chicken into smaller pieces using a large sharp knife or a meat cleaver.

2. Pound the red chillies, coriander and garlic together in a pestle and mortar.

3. Heat the oil in a wok and fry the chicken until golden and almost cooked through. Remove from the pan.

4. Add the pounded up chillies and fry for a few minutes. Return chicken to the pan and add the green chillies, fish sauce and oyster sauce, if using. Cook over a medium heat for 5-10 minutes or until the chicken is completely cooked.

5. Stir in the basil leaves and serve garnished with chilli 'flowers'.

TIME: Preparation takes 20 minutes and cooking takes 20 minutes.

COOK'S TIP: Tearing basil leaves actually allows more flavour to develop in the dish than cutting them with a knife.

PREPARATION: If coriander with roots is unavailable, use the stems only.

YELLOW CHICKEN CURRY

This easy-to-prepare curry illustrates the Indian influence on traditional Thai cuisine.

SERVES 4

460g/1lb chicken breast, skinned and boned
2 tbsps oil
2 cloves garlic, sliced
1 onion, peeled and cut into wedges
3 tbsps yellow curry paste (see separate recipe)
570ml/1 pint thick coconut milk
1 small potato, peeled and cut into chunks
2 kaffir lime leaves, shredded

1. Cut the chicken into even-sized chunks.

2. Heat the oil in a wok and fry the garlic and onion for 3 minutes, then stir in the curry paste and fry for 1 minute.

3. Stir in half the coconut milk and bring to the boil. Boil rapidly for 5 minutes, stirring occasionally. Stir in the remaining coconut milk, bring to the boil and add the potato and chicken.

4. Reduce the heat and simmer gently for 20-30 minutes or until the chicken is cooked and the potato is tender.

5. Spoon into serving dishes and sprinkle with the shredded lime leaves.

TIME: Preparation takes 10 minutes, and cooking takes 30-40 minutes.

BUYING GUIDE: Fresh or dried Kaffir lime leaves are available from Asian food stores. If not available substitute strips of lime zest.

SERVING IDEA: Accompany with Thai Steamed Rice or Stir-Fried Thai Noodles.

BARBECUED CHICKEN

These spicy chicken pieces are served with a hot dipping sauce.

SERVES 4-6

680g/1½lbs chicken thighs
2 tbsps red curry paste (see separate recipe)
2 cloves garlic, crushed
140ml/¼ pint thick coconut milk
2 tbsps chopped fresh coriander leaves,
     stem and root

Dipping Sauce
1 small red chilli, sliced
1 small green chilli, sliced
60ml/4 tbsps white wine vinegar

Garnish
Banana leaves
Chilli halves

1. Place the chicken in a mixing bowl.

2. Combine together the red curry paste, garlic, coconut milk and coriander and pour over the chicken. Toss together until all the chicken pieces are well coated. Leave to marinate for 2 hours.

3. Combine the sliced chillies and vinegar for the dipping sauce and set aside until required.

4. Cook the chicken pieces over a medium hot barbecue or under a preheated grill for about 10 minutes or until tender and cooked through. Turn frequently and baste with any remaining marinade.

5. Serve hot or cold with the dipping sauce. Garnish with shapes cut from a banana leaf and chilli halves.

TIME: Preparation takes 10 minutes, plus 2 hours marinating. Cooking takes 10-15 minutes.

SERVING IDEAS: Accompany with rice and a green paw paw salad. To make the paw paw salad shred or grate unripe paw paw and mix with lime juice, chillies and a little fish sauce and sugar.

SPICY MINCED CHICKEN

*This version of a traditional Thai dish comes from the North-East of Thailand,
and contains glutinous rice which gives it a delicious nutty texture.*

SERVES 4

2 tbsps glutinous rice
2 tbsps oil
2 cloves garlic, crushed
6 small red or green chillies, sliced
340g/12oz minced chicken
1 tbsp oyster sauce
1 tbsp fish sauce
1 tsp salted black beans
2 tbsps soy sauce

Garnish
Spring onion slices

1. Place the rice in a wok and dry-fry for 5-10 minutes until the grains are golden on all sides, shaking the wok as it cooks.

2. Pour the roasted rice into a pestle and mortar and pound until ground almost to a powder.

3. Heat the oil in the wok and fry the garlic and chillies for 2-3 minutes until softened.

4. Add the chicken and stir-fry, breaking the chicken up as it cooks.

5. Once the chicken is cooked and no longer pink, stir in the oyster sauce, fish sauce, black beans and soy sauce.

6. Add the ground rice and stir-fry for 2-3 minutes.

7. Serve immediately, sprinkled with spring onion slices.

TIME: Preparation takes 15 minutes, and cooking takes 25-30 minutes.

COOK'S TIP: If you don't have a pestle and mortar, put the rice into a plastic bag and crush with a rolling pin.

BUYING GUIDE: Glutinous or 'sticky' rice as it is sometimes called has a high gluten content, and when cooked it forms a sticky mass. It is available from Asian food stores in both long- and short-grain types.

STIR-FRIED CHICKEN WITH GINGER

A popular Thai dish served in many restaurants.

SERVES 4

2 tbsps oil
2 cloves garlic, crushed
2 shallots, chopped
340g/12oz skinned and boned chicken
    breast, cut into thin strips
5cm/2-inch piece fresh root ginger, peeled
    and cut into shreds
2 Kaffir lime leaves, shredded
60g/2oz whole blanched almonds
120g/4oz long or French beans, cut into
    5cm/2-inch lengths
1 red pepper, cut into strips
90g/3oz water chestnuts, sliced
3 tbsps fish sauce
1 tbsp sugar

1. Heat the oil in a wok and fry the garlic and shallots until beginning to soften. Add the chicken and fry until it changes colour.

2. Add the ginger, lime leaves, almonds, beans, pepper and water chestnuts. Stir-fry, tossing the ingredients frequently, for 5 minutes until vegetables are cooked but still crisp.

3. Stir in the fish sauce and sugar and serve with rice or noodles.

TIME: Preparation takes 15 minutes and cooking takes 10 minutes.

COOK'S TIP: Cut the chicken across the grain to keep it tender.

VARIATION: Use unsalted cashew nuts in place of the almonds.

THAI STEAMED RICE

Thai jasmine rice is a fragrant rice with a delicate flavour. Do not add salt during cooking as this will destroy the slightly nutty flavour.

SERVES 4-6

225g/8oz jasmine rice
570ml/1 pint water

1. Rinse the rice under running water and drain.

2. Place the rice and the measured water in a saucepan and bring gently to the boil.

3. Stir the rice, cover, reduce the heat and simmer gently for 10 minutes or until the water has been absorbed.

4. Line a steamer with a piece of muslin and pile the rice into the steamer. Steam the rice over gently simmering water for 30 minutes.

5. Stand the rice for a few minutes, then fluff up with a fork before serving.

TIME: Preparation takes 5 minutes and cooking takes about 40 minutes.

SERVING IDEA: Use this rice to accompany a Thai curry.

SHRIMP PASTE FRIED RICE

A strongly flavoured rice dish. Serve with vegetables such as steamed or stir-fried bok choy.

SERVES 4

2 tbsps oil
30g/1oz dried shrimps
4 cloves garlic, crushed
2 red chillies, seeded and chopped
680g/1½lbs cooked rice
2 tbsps shrimp paste
2 eggs, beaten
4 spring onions, sliced
3 tbsps fish sauce

Garnish
Coriander leaves

1. Heat the oil in a wok and fry the shrimps for about 30 seconds; remove and set aside to drain on kitchen paper.

2. Add the garlic and chillies and fry briefly until softened.

3. Stir in the rice and shrimp paste and stir-fry for 5 minutes or until heated through.

4. Add the beaten egg and spring onions and cook over a low heat, stirring until the egg is cooked.

5. Sprinkle with the fish sauce. Serve sprinkled with the dried shrimps and garnished with coriander leaves.

TIME: Preparation takes about 10 minutes and cooking takes 15 minutes.

BUYING GUIDE: Dried shrimps and shrimp paste can be bought in packets from Asian food stores. Once the packets are opened, keep stored in an airtight container as they both have a very pungent smell.

SPICY RICE WITH CHICKEN

This spicy rice dish can also be served as a light supper dish.

SERVES 4

225g/8oz cooked chicken
120g/4oz long beans or French beans, cut
    into 2.5cm/1-inch lengths
1 tbsp oil
2 tbsps red curry paste (see separate recipe)
460g/1lb cooked rice
2 tbsps fish sauce
1 tsp palm sugar

Garnish
Chilli 'flowers' (see Beef Sate:
    PREPARATION)
Spring onions

1. Cut the chicken into thin shreds. Blanch the beans in boiling water for 5 minutes or until just tender.

2. Heat the oil in a wok and fry the curry paste for 3-4 minutes, stirring frequently.

3. Add the chicken and rice to the wok and stir-fry for 5 minutes, tossing frequently.

4. Add the beans and cook a further 2 minutes or until all the ingredients are piping hot.

5. Mix together the fish sauce and sugar, stir until the sugar dissolves. Add to the wok. Toss well and serve garnished with chilli 'flowers' and spring onions.

TIME: Preparation takes 10 minutes and cooking takes about 15 minutes.

VARIATION: If palm sugar is unavailable substitute muscovado sugar.

BUYING GUIDE: Ready-made red curry paste can be bought from some large supermarkets and Asian food stores. Palm sugar can also be bought from Asian food stores.

BAKED PINEAPPLE RICE

An attractively presented dish from Bangkok and the central plains.

SERVES 6

1 ripe pineapple
2 tbsps oil
1 clove garlic, crushed
4 shallots, chopped
1 tbsp yellow curry paste (see separate
    recipe)
460g/1lb cooked rice
140ml/¼ pint thick coconut milk
60g/2oz raisins
60g/2oz toasted cashew nuts

Garnish
Chilli 'flowers' (see Beef Sate:
    PREPARATION)

1. Cut the pineapple in half lengthwise, keeping the leaves attached. Scoop out the flesh using a tablespoon and a paring knife, to leave two shells with a thin border of flesh attached. Chop half the flesh to use later in the dish, the remaining pineapple is not needed for this recipe.

2. Heat the oil in a wok and fry the garlic and shallots until softened. Stir in the curry paste and fry for 1 minute.

3. Add the rice and toss together with the shallot mixture. Stir in the coconut milk, raisins, chopped pineapple and cashew nuts.

4. Pile the rice mixture into the pineapple shells. Wrap the pineapple leaves in foil to prevent them from burning and place on a baking sheet.

5. Bake in an oven preheated to 160°C/325°F/Gas Mark 3, for 20 minutes. Remove from the foil and serve garnished with chilli 'flowers'.

TIME: Preparation takes 20 minutes and cooking takes about 25 minutes.

COOK'S TIP: If the pineapple shells won't stand stable, cut a thin slice from the underneath.

PREPARATION: For thick coconut milk stir the contents of the canned milk together before using or make up from instant coconut milk following the manufacturer's instructions.

Tofu with Crispy Noodles

Tofu is made from soya beans and is available from health food stores and large supermarkets. It is ideal for making vegetarian main courses.

SERVES 4

Oil, for deep frying
120g/4oz rice noodles (vermicelli)
225g/8oz tofu, drained and patted dry
2 carrots, peeled and sliced
90g/3oz broccoli, divided into small florets
2 sticks celery, sliced
1 onion, peeled and cut into wedges
1 tsp shrimp paste
2 tbsps light soy sauce
3 tbsps white wine vinegar
2 tbsps soft dark muscovado sugar
1 tsp grated fresh root ginger

1. Heat the oil to 180°C/350°F in a wok. Add the rice noodles in small batches, turn over and fry for a few seconds. The rice will puff up immediately.

2. Remove from the oil and drain well on kitchen paper.

3. Cut the tofu into cubes and fry for a few minutes until browned on all sides, remove from the oil and set aside.

4. Pour off most of the oil, add the carrot, broccoli, celery and onion to the wok and stir-fry for 2 minutes or until the vegetables are cooked but still crisp.

5. Stir in the shrimp paste, soy sauce, vinegar, sugar and ginger. Return the vermicelli and tofu to the wok, toss to mix and serve immediately.

TIME: Preparation takes 10 minutes and cooking takes 10 minutes.

BUYING GUIDE: Shrimp paste, known as Kapi in Thailand, is a strong tasting seasoning made from dried salted shrimps. Store in an airtight jar as its smell is very pungent.

VARIATION: Use smoked tofu for a different flavour.

STIR-FRIED THAI NOODLES

This is a well known basic Thai dish with as many variations as there are Thai cooks.

SERVES 4

175g/6oz rice noodles
60ml/4 tbsps oil
225g/8oz tofu, cut into cubes
3 cloves garlic, crushed
60g/2oz dried shrimps
3 tbsps chopped pickled turnip
60ml/4 tbsps fish sauce
30g/1oz palm sugar
1 tbsp soy sauce
2 tbsps tamarind juice
2 eggs, beaten
1 tbsp chopped garlic chives
60g/2oz roasted peanuts, chopped
225g/8oz bean sprouts

Garnish
Chilli strips

1. Soak the rice noodles in boiling water for 10-15 minutes or until softened; drain and set aside.

2. Heat the oil in a wok and stir-fry the tofu until browned on all sides. Remove with a slotted spoon and set aside.

3. Add the garlic and shrimps and stir-fry for 2 minutes. Reduce the heat and add the noodles. Cook for 5 minutes, tossing frequently. Add the pickled turnip, fish sauce, sugar, soy and tamarind juice and cook for 2 minutes.

4. Add the beaten egg and cook, tossing the ingredients together until the egg sets. Stir in the tofu, garlic chives, peanuts and bean sprouts. Serve immediately.

TIME: Preparation takes 10 minutes, plus 10-15 minutes soaking time. Cooking takes about 15 minutes.

PREPARATION: See recipe for Fried Fish with Tamarind for method of preparing tamarind juice. If tamarind is unavailable, substitute lemon juice.

BUYING GUIDE: Pickled turnip is available from Asian food stores. Garlic chives, also known as ku chai are sometimes available in large supermarkets. If unavailable substitute ordinary chives and a little extra garlic.

CHAING MAI NOODLES

Originally from Burma, this dish has evolved to have a distinct Thai flavour.

SERVES 4-6

2 tbsps oil

2 cloves garlic, crushed

4 shallots, chopped

1 tbsp red curry paste (see separate recipe)

½ tsp ground turmeric

Pinch ground cumin

Pinch ground coriander

280ml/½ pint coconut milk

225g/8oz rump or sirloin steak, thinly sliced

75ml/5 tbsps fish sauce

60g/2oz palm sugar

1 tbsp soy sauce

2 tbsps lime juice

1 tbsp garlic chives, chopped

460g/1lb fresh egg noodles

Garnish

Chilli 'flowers' (see Beef Sate:
    PREPARATION)

Crispy egg noodles, optional

1. Heat the oil in a wok and fry the garlic and shallots until softened.

2. Stir in the red curry paste, turmeric, cumin and coriander. Stir-fry for 1 minute.

3. Add the coconut milk and bring to the boil, reduce the heat and add the beef. Simmer for 15-20 minutes or until the beef is cooked.

4. Stir in the fish sauce, sugar, soy, lime juice and garlic chives.

5. Meanwhile, cook the egg noodles in boiling water for 1 minute. Drain and arrange on a serving dish. Spoon the beef curry on top and serve garnished with chilli 'flowers' and crispy noodles, if wished.

TIME: Preparation takes 20 minutes, and cooking takes about 20 minutes.

COOK'S TIP: Cut the steak across the grain to keep it tender.

PREPARATION: To make the noodle garnish, deep-fry a few cooked egg noodles until crispy.

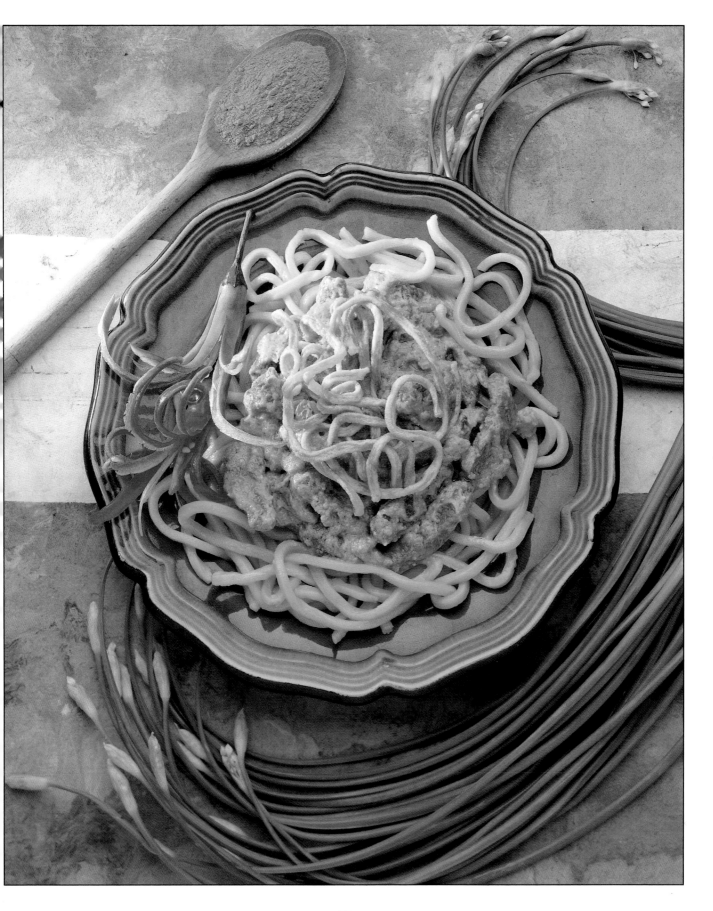

THAI RICE SALAD

A delicious and attractive salad from Southern Thailand.

SERVES 4

340g/12oz cooked rice
1 grapefruit,
½ cucumber
6 spring onions
2.5cm/1-inch piece fresh root ginger
60g/2oz shredded coconut
60g/2oz bean sprouts
60g/2oz dried shrimps, chopped
2 stems lemon grass, soft core thinly sliced

Sauce
120ml/4 fl oz fish sauce
60ml/4 tbsps lime juice
2 tbsps light muscovado sugar

---

1. Divide the rice into four and press a quarter of it into a ramekin dish or tea cup. Turn out onto a serving plate. Repeat with the remaining rice.

2. Cut off all the peel and pith from the grapefruit, then remove the segments of flesh by cutting in between the membranes.

3. Cut the cucumber into quarters and slice thinly. Slice the spring onions diagonally. Peel the ginger and cut into thin shreds.

4. Arrange all the different salad ingredients separately on a serving platter.

5. Combine the ingredients for the sauce and pour into one large or four small dishes.

6. To serve; each diner should scatter some of the individual ingredients over their mound of rice then drizzle the sauce over the top.

TIME: Preparation takes 20 minutes.

VARIATION: The salad ingredients can be mixed together and tossed in the sauce just before serving.

CUCUMBER SALAD

Salads are an important part of a Thai meal. They are usually carefully arranged rather than simply tossed together.

SERVES 4

1 cucumber
Few salad leaves, washed
1 red pepper, sliced
30g/1oz roasted peanuts

Dressing
2 tbsps lime juice
1 tbsp fish sauce
1 tsp sugar
1 small red or green chilli, seeded and
    chopped
2 tsps chopped fresh coriander leaves

1. Cut the cucumber in half lengthwise and scoop out the seeds.

2. Cut the cucumber into slices about 5mm/ ¼-inch thick.

3. Arrange the lettuce leaves on a serving plate and then scatter the pepper around the edge. Pile the cucumber into the centre. Sprinkle with roasted peanuts.

4. To make the dressing, whisk all the ingredients together with a fork or place in a small screw-top jar and shake well.

5. Just before serving drizzle the dressing over the salad.

TIME: Preparation takes 10 minutes.

COOK'S TIP: Do not add the dressing to the salad until serving time.

TOFU SALAD

This dish can also be served hot, return the tofu to the wok and heat through, then serve immediately.

SERVES 4

90ml/6 tbsps oil
225g/8oz tofu, cubed
2 cloves garlic, crushed
120g/4oz broccoli florets
120g/4oz mange tout peas
1 tbsp soy sauce
1 tsp salted black beans
½ tsp palm sugar
90ml/6 tbsps vegetable stock
½ tsp cornflour

1. Heat the oil in a wok and fry the tofu until golden on all sides. Remove with a slotted spoon and place in the refrigerator until required.

2. Pour off most of the oil. Add the garlic and fry until softened. Stir in the broccoli and mange tout, and stir-fry until just tender.

3. Add the soy, black beans and sugar and fry 1 minute.

4. Mix a little of the stock with the cornflour and add the remaining stock and cornflour mixture to the wok. Cook until sauce thickens slightly.

5. Transfer to a serving dish and chill. To serve, scatter the tofu cubes over the cooked vegetables.

TIME: Preparation takes 15 minutes and cooking takes about 10 minutes.

BUYING GUIDE: Salted black beans can be bought in Asian food stores. They are often sold in small quantities in plastic bags, and should be stored in an airtight container.

MIXED VEGETABLE STIR-FRY

Very fresh vegetables cooked quickly and simply play a large part in Thai cuisine as this dish shows.

SERVES 4

Prik Dong
6 red or green chillies
90ml/6 tbsps white wine vinegar

2 tbsps oil
3 cloves garlic, crushed
1 shallot, sliced
90g/3oz each cauliflower and broccoli
   divided into small florets
1 small red pepper, sliced
120g/4oz mange tout peas
120g/4oz baby corn cobs
120g/4oz long beans or French beans, cut
   into 5cm/2-inch lengths
2 carrots, peeled and sliced
90g/3oz fresh or canned straw mushrooms
2 tsps palm sugar
1 tbsp light soy sauce

1. Slice the chillies diagonally and combine with the vinegar to serve as a dipping sauce for the vegetables.

2. Heat the oil in a wok and add all the vegetables at once.

3. Stir-fry for 4 minutes until the vegetables are cooked but still crisp.

4. Stir the sugar into the soy sauce and add to the wok, toss well and serve. Serve with the dipping sauce.

TIME: Preparation takes 15 minutes and cooking takes 4-6 minutes.

COOK'S TIP: Use the dipping sauce with noodles as well as vegetables.

BUYING GUIDE: Long beans are also known as yard-long beans because of their excessive length. Substitute French beans if unavailable.

SAUTÉED BEAN SPROUTS

A simple vegetable dish which can be served with a hot dipping sauce if wished, or as a foil to a hot curry.

SERVES 4

2 tbsps oil
8 spring onions, thickly sliced
340g/12oz bean sprouts, rinsed and drained
120g/4oz cooked, peeled prawns (optional)
½ small head of Chinese cabbage, shredded
1 tbsp fish sauce

1. Heat the oil in a wok until sizzling then add the spring onions, bean sprouts and prawns, if using. Stir-fry for 1-2 minutes.

2. Add the Chinese cabbage and toss over a high heat for about 1 minute or until just beginning to wilt.

3. Stir in the fish sauce and serve immediately with a dipping sauce of your choice.

TIME: Preparation takes 5 minutes and cooking takes 5 minutes.

COOK'S TIP: Use fresh bean sprouts rather than canned for this recipe, if possible.

STIR-FRIED BABY CORN WITH MUSHROOMS

Serve as a vegetable dish as part of a complete Thai meal.

SERVES 4

2 tbsps oil
2 cloves garlic, crushed
4 shallots, chopped
460g/1lb baby corn, cut in half lengthways
120g/4oz mange tout peas
225g/8oz canned straw mushrooms
　　(drained weight)
1 tbsp grated galangal
½ tsp dried chilli flakes
1 tbsp fish sauce
1 tbsp soy sauce

1. Heat the oil in a wok and fry the garlic and shallots until softened.

2. Stir in the baby corn and cook for 5 minutes, add the mange tout and continue cooking for 2 minutes.

3. Stir in the mushrooms, galangal and chilli and stir-fry for 2 minutes. Sprinkle with the fish sauce and soy sauce and serve.

TIME: Preparation takes 10 minutes and cooking takes about 10 minutes.

BUYING GUIDE: Fresh galangal and powdered galangal, often called Laos, is available in Asian food stores. If unavailable, substitute fresh root ginger.

NUOC CHAM

Delicious served with rice or Spicy Prawn Wraps.

SERVES 4

1 tbsp lime juice
60ml/4 tbsps fish sauce
3 tbsps water
1 tsp palm sugar
1 red chilli, seeded and shredded
1 tbsp grated carrot
1 tbsp chopped roasted peanuts

1. Combine the lime juice, fish sauce and water in a small bowl and stir in the sugar. Stir until the sugar dissolves.

2. Add the chilli and grated carrot, then stir in the roasted peanuts.

3. Serve over rice or with many other Thai dishes.

TIME: Preparation takes 5 minutes.

COOK'S TIP: This sauce is best served freshly made.

FISH SAUCE WITH CHILLI

As well as being used as a dipping sauce, this can be added to curries and stir-fries to give spiciness and saltiness to the dish.

SERVES 4

60ml/4 tbsps fish sauce
1 tbsp lime juice
½ tsp palm sugar
6 small green chillies, sliced into rings
½ small shallot, finely chopped

1. Combine the fish sauce and lime juice together in a small bowl.

2. Add the sugar and stir until the sugar dissolves.

3. Add the prepared chillies and shallot and stir until well combined. Leave to stand for at least 30 minutes before using.

TIME: Preparation takes 5 minutes, plus at least 30 minutes standing time.

SERVING IDEAS: Pour over steamed or fried rice.

Sweet Chilli Sauce

A delicious tangy sweet and sour sauce.

SERVES 4

120g/4oz canned plums (drained weight), stoned
1 tbsp oil
3 red chillies, chopped
1 clove garlic, crushed
1 tsp palm sugar
2 tbsps white wine vinegar
Fish sauce, to taste

1. Chop the plums very finely, this can be done in a food processor if preferred.

2. Heat the oil in a wok or small pan and fry the chillies and garlic for 3 minutes, until just softened.

3. Stir in the remaining ingredients and heat through.

TIME: Preparation takes 10 minutes.

SERVING IDEAS: Serve with Spring Rolls or other similar Thai dishes.

Sweet and Sour Dipping Sauce

Another popular dipping sauce that can be served with a lot of Thai dishes.

SERVES 4

60g/2oz cucumber
30g/1oz carrot
140ml/¼ pint white wine vinegar
60g/2oz palm sugar
1 tsp chopped fresh coriander, leaves and stems

1. Cut the cucumber into very small dice.

2. Peel the carrot and cut into very small dice.

3. Combine all the ingredients in a bowl and stir until the sugar dissolves.

TIME: Preparation takes 10 minutes.

COOK'S TIP: If palm sugar is unavailable, substitute muscovado sugar.

YELLOW CURRY PASTE

MAKES 75-90ml/5-6 tbsps

2 tbsps cumin seeds
2 tbsps coriander seeds
3 stems lemon grass, chopped
1 tbsp grated fresh root ginger
6 red chillies, seeded and chopped
1 tsp salt
3 cloves garlic, crushed
1 small shallot, finely chopped
1 tsp ground turmeric
1 tsp shrimp paste

1. Place the cumin and coriander seeds in a wok or frying pan without any oil and dry-fry for 3-4 minutes, shaking the pan frequently to prevent the spices from burning. Remove from the heat and set aside.

2. Place the lemon grass and ginger in a large pestle and mortar and pound together until well crushed. Add the chillies and salt and continue pounding together for about 4 minutes.

3. Add the garlic and shallot and pound until broken down, then add the fried spices and turmeric. Finally add the shrimp paste and continue to pound together until a smooth moist paste is produced.

4. Store in a small air-tight jar in the refrigerator until required. The paste will keep for up to 1 month.

TIME: Preparation takes 15 minutes.

PREPARATION: Remove the tough outer leaves of the lemon grass and chop only the soft inner core.

NAM PRIK

This is a hot dipping sauce, which can be served with most Thai dishes.

SERVES 4

1 tsp shrimp paste
1 tsp salt
1 tsp light brown sugar
4 cloves garlic, crushed
5 small red chillies, chopped
8 canned anchovy fillets, chopped
1 tbsp light soy sauce
Juice of ½ lime

1. Pound the shrimp paste, salt, sugar, garlic, chillies and anchovies to a smooth paste in a pestle and mortar or mini food processor.

2. Stir in the soy sauce and lime juice and transfer to a small serving dish.

GREEN AND RED CURRY PASTES

Red and green curry pastes are the basis of most Thai curries. Red curry paste is milder than the green.

MAKES 45-60ml/3-4 tbsps of each

Green Curry Paste

16 green Serrano or other small chillies, chopped

3 cloves garlic, crushed

2 stems lemon grass, roughly chopped

3 spring onions, chopped

1 tsp grated fresh root ginger

1 tsp coriander seeds

1 tsp caraway seeds

4 whole cloves

1 tsp ground nutmeg

1 tsp shrimp paste

3 tbsps oil

Red Curry Paste

12 small red chillies, chopped

3 cloves garlic, crushed

1 stem lemon grass, chopped

1 small onion, finely chopped

1 tsp grated fresh root ginger

2 tsps chopped fresh coriander stems and root

Large pinch cumin

1 tsp shrimp paste

2 tbsps oil

1. To make either the green or red curry paste, place the chillies, garlic, lemon grass and onions in a pestle and mortar and pound until the mixture is well bruised and the juices begin to blend.

2. Add all the remaining ingredients except the oil and continue to pound until a paste is formed.

3. Finally blend in the oil.

4. The curry pastes can also be made in a mini food processor (the quantity is too small for a full size blender or processor). Place all the ingredients in the processor and grind to a paste.

5. Store in a small air-tight jar in the refrigerator until required. The paste will keep for up to 1 month.

TIME: Preparation takes 15 minutes for each paste.

PREPARATION: When using lemon grass, remove the tough outer leaves first and chop only the soft central core.

BUYING GUIDE: Shrimp paste is available from Asian food stores. Store in an air-tight container.

THAI FRUIT PLATTER WITH COCONUT SAUCE

Usually a Thai meal will finish with fresh fruit. Here we serve a selection of fruit with a simple coconut sauce.

SERVES 4

Selection of Thai fruit such as

Lychees
Rambutans
Mango
Pineapple
Watermelon
Honey dew melon
Papaya
Star fruit
Bananas

Coconut Sauce

175ml/6fl oz thick coconut milk
60g/2oz caster sugar

1. Prepare the fruit; peel lychees or rambutans, starting at the stem end.

2. Cut mango in half either side of the large cental stone, peel and slice the flesh into fingers.

3. Cut the pineapple in to wedges, peeled if wished.

4. Cut the melons and papaya in half and discard the seeds. Peel and slice.

5. Slice the star fruit.

6. Cut bananas diagonally into chunks and toss in lemon juice.

7. Arrange the fruit on a serving platter.

8. Make the sauce by combining the coconut milk and sugar. Pour over the fruit or serve in a bowl or jug.

TIME: Preparation takes 30 minutes.

COOK'S TIP: Chill the fruit before serving if wished.

MANGO ICE CREAM

*The cool, smooth, creaminess of this delicious ice cream makes it the perfect
end to a Thai meal.*

SERVES 8

420ml/¾ pint thick coconut milk
3 egg yolks
60g/4 tbsps sugar
280ml/½ pint double cream
3 ripe mangoes, peeled and stoned

Decoration
Toasted flaked almonds

1. Heat the coconut milk in a saucepan until very hot, but not boiling.

2. Beat together the egg yolks and sugar in a bowl, add a few spoons of the hot coconut milk and stir well.

3. Stir into the remaining coconut milk and cook over a saucepan of simmering water, stirring constantly until it coats the back of a spoon.

4. Remove from the heat and cool. Whip the double cream until soft peaks form, then stir in the cooled custard.

5. Chop a little of the mango into small pieces and purée the remainder in a food processor or push through a sieve.

6. Fold the mango purée and chopped mango into the custard. Pour into a shallow, freezer-proof dish and freeze until slushy.

7. Remove from the freezer and process in a food processor or beat with an electric whisk until smooth. Freeze and beat once more then transfer to a freezer container and freeze until solid.

8. Remove the ice cream to the refrigerator about 30 minutes before serving.

9. Scoop into dishes and serve sprinkled with toasted flaked almonds.

TIME: Preparation takes 30 minutes and cooking takes 10 minutes.

COOK'S TIP: Beating the ice cream as it is freezing breaks up the ice crystals and makes the texture of the ice cream smoother.

PREPARATION: Do not allow the coconut milk mixture to boil.

STICKY RICE WITH MANGO AND STAR FRUIT

Sweet, glutinous rice is served in many forms as a dessert in Thailand, and this delicious version is served with mango and star fruit.

SERVES 4

225g/8oz glutinous or 'sticky' rice
420ml/¾ pint thick coconut milk
90g/3oz sugar
Pinch salt
1 mango
1 star fruit

1. Soak the rice overnight in cold water.

2. Line the top of a steamer with muslin. Drain the rice and place in the steamer, cover and steam for 25 minutes. The rice will be just tender but not fully cooked.

3. Combine the coconut milk, sugar and salt in a saucepan and heat gently. Stir in the steamed rice and simmer for 2 minutes.

4. Remove from the heat, cover and leave to stand for 15 minutes. The rice will continue to cook in this time.

5. Cut the mango in half as close to the large central stone as possible. Remove the peel, and slice the flesh. Slice the star fruit.

6. Arrange the fruit and rice attractively on serving dishes.

TIME: Preparation takes 10 minutes, plus overnight soaking. Cooking takes 27 minutes, plus 15 minutes standing.

COOK'S TIP: Serve this dish with any other exotic fruit you like.

BUYING GUIDE: Glutinous rice is a special type of rice that cooks to a very sticky consistency, hence its name. It is rather cloudy in appearance and is available from Asian stores in both short- and long-grain varieties.

THAI COCONUT CUSTARDS

One of the best known and most loved of Thai desserts.

SERVES 6

4 eggs
420ml/¾ pint thick coconut milk
120g/4oz caster sugar
½ tsp jasmine water

To decorate
Desiccated coconut, toasted
Lime zest
Lime twists

1. Place the eggs, coconut milk, sugar and jasmine water in a bowl and whisk together until slightly frothy.

2. Pour into a shallow dish, that will fit into the top of a steamer.

3. Steam slowly over gently simmering water for 30-40 minutes until just set. If the custard cooks too quickly, it will be rubbery in texture.

4. Remove from the steamer and allow to cool. Cut into wedges or blocks and decorate with coconut and grated lime zest and lime twists.

TIME: Preparation takes 5 minutes, cooking takes 30-40 minutes.

PREPARATION: The custard is cooked when the tip of a knife blade inserted into the centre comes out clean.

BUYING GUIDE: Jasmine water, known as mali in Thailand, is made from the flowers of the shrub and is available in Asian food stores.

BLACK STICKY RICE

Look out for the rice in Thai or Oriental food stores. Substitute white sticky rice if the black type is unavailable.

SERVES 6

175g/6oz black glutinous rice
1.1 litres/2 pints water
150g/5oz granulated sugar
420ml/¾ pint thick coconut milk
90g/3oz grated fresh coconut flesh

1. Rinse the rice under plenty of running water and drain.

2. Place the rice in a large saucepan with the water. Bring gently to the boil. Stir and reduce the heat, then simmer for 45 minutes or until rice is tender, stirring occasionally.

3. If the rice is tender and any water is left, drain off and discard. If the rice is not tender but there is not enough water add a little more and continue until rice is cooked.

4. Stir in 90g/3oz of the sugar and 280ml/½ pint of the coconut milk, simmer gently for 10 minutes.

5. Combine the remaining sugar, coconut milk and coconut flesh in a small pan and heat gently.

6. Spoon the rice into serving bowls and top with the coconut mixture. Serve at once.

TIME: Preparation takes 15 minutes, and cooking takes 55 minutes.

VARIATION: To make chocolate sticky rice add cocoa powder, to taste, with the coconut milk and sugar in step 4.

Index